SOCCER FUNDAMENTALS FOR PLAYERS AND COACHES

Wiel Coerver

PRENTICE HALL
Englewood Cliffs, New Jersey 07632

Library of Congress Cataloging-in-Publication Data

ISBN 0-13-815226-8

10 9 8 7 6 5 - 4

Title of the original work: Leerplan voor de ideale voetballer.

Author of the original work: Wiel Coerver

Text editor of the original work: Johan Derksen

Photographs of the original work: Robert Collette

Avcknowledgment

American edition published with the assistance of Expersport—Haarlem.

ISBN 0-13-815226-8

PRENTICE HALL
Career & Personal Development
Englewood Cliffs, NJ 07632
A Simon & Schuster Company

On the World Wide Web at http://www.phdirect.com

Prentice-Hall International (UK) Limited, *London*
Prentice-Hall of Australia Pty. Limited, *Sydney*
Prentice-Hall Canada Inc., *Toronto*
Prentice-Hall Hispanoamericana, S.A., *Mexico*
Prentice-Hall of India Private Limited, *New Delhi*
Prentice-Hall of Japan, Inc., *Tokyo*
Simon & Schuster Asia Pte. Ltd., *Singapore*
Editora Prentice-Hall do Brasil, Ltda., *Rio de Janeiro*

SOCCER FUNDAMENTALS FOR PLAYERS AND COACHES

Table of Contents

The Ideal
Soccer Player

Technical training.

There is a need for technical training

Winning teams need more than technically accomplished, predictable players. Fans don't flock to soccer stadiums to watch impersonal ball passing. Matthews, Di Stefano, Pele, Eusebio, Best, and the many other soccer greats—individuals with unique personalities and compelling drives to win—*they* are the reason for the once-filled soccer stadiums.

Soccer personalities are disappearing. There are fewer and fewer goal-scorers and players with innovative plays or creative abilities. Yet innovation, creativity, and the ability to improvise are essential to competitive soccer. It's the single player with that "something extra" who will make the crowd sit up when he gains possession of the ball. And it's that something extra—that spark of original fielding and burst of creative energy—that can mean the difference between a good team and a great team, a comfortable win-loss and a winning season.

ATTACKING ABILITIES— KEY TO COMPETITIVE SOCCER

Most coaches stick to unrealistic training programs that concentrate on defensive fitness at the expense of offensive attacking techniques. Even coaches who emphasize "competitive soccer" often prefer not to allow their players to engage in individual play for fear that they might lose possession of the ball. As a result, it is rare to find a training program that encourages individual attacking techniques. Instead, you find players running over the field like members of a herd; the coach gives a signal with his whistle, and the players break into yet another precision sprint.

Naturally, game training is a must: three against two, four against three, five against five, and so on. These are useful positional techniques for players who have mastered how to attack. But it is the attack technique that must be mastered first, so that when a player gets possession he is capable of more than just passing the ball and resorting to kick-and-run soccer.

Training of Young Players

Young and inexperienced players seldom get possession of the ball; they spend most of the time running after their opponent. Even if they did gain possession, they would be unable to attack aggressively because they haven't mastered the basic moves.

There is far too little ball contact in training programs for young players. There is not much point in practicing kicking or trapping until the players have a feel for the ball and can bring it under control with any part of the body. The very young should not be troubled with planned training and assignments. Let them carry on as they are, so that they can learn to cope with the ball naturally. Team play is not an issue; young children are concerned only with the ball and the goal. Schedule group games rather than real matches. This will allow for more ball handling. Youngsters should also be encouraged to learn from the ball-handling techniques of the professional soccer greats. Yet this is seldom done.

Without proper technical training consistently and early in life, few soccer players will rise above the "average" level.

Technical Training

Technical training is a matter of constant repetition until a particular technique has been completely mastered. Every coach in a specialized sport seems to be aware of this fundamental rule—except soccer coaches, who tend to emphasize the physiological aspects of playing. The physiological aspects of training are important, but it's the physical training—the hours of practice and repetition—that will help players learn to play soccer.

Coaches also rarely schedule "homework" for their young players. Having players practice on their own what was covered during a team workout helps reinforce the newly learned skills and promotes both confidence and creativity.

Inner Stimulation

Inappropriate exercise and the failure to concentrate on technical shortcomings can result in inadequate tactical development, but even worse, it can dampen the spirits of players. State of mind plays a crucial part in any organized sport, and soccer is no exception. A player's state of mind can have a positive influence on his performance, and success produces a

Young players long for technical training.

Outside practice
is important

particularly agreeable feeling in most people! Spending excessive training time on running and other nonspecific exercises won't help your players develop the most important quality—motivation. Young players are thirsty for their chance to succeed and are more than willing to learn. Yet they re seldom given the chance to practice techniques to which they can devote themselves heart and soul. Their ambition, inspiration, and dedication are undermined, and they lose interest in playing soccer. It's up to you, the coach, to keep that inner stimulation and drive to succeed in your players.

The Coach

There are many kinds of coaches, but few who are willing to concentrate on the basics of technical training. Coaches are human. They cannot turn mediocre players into superstars. Practical training sessions are, of course, important, but they should not concentrate only on defensive strategies. Circuit and condition training are no longer enough; the sport of soccer can only be rejuvenated by encouraging your players to work on their offensive moves and learning to think independently as well as part of a team.

DEVELOPING A SUCCESSFUL TRAINING PLAN

Only the best players are capable of exciting the public. The training plan presented here is geared to the specific qualities of those players. It makes it possible to deliberately set out to become a player with abilities far above the average. At first, you will devote all your energies to helping your promising players become as gifted individually as the more established top players. Then you apply these techniques in practice competitions, with group games and matches, to further develop your players' tactical skills.

This plan is intended for players who wish to master as many techniques as possible and have the mentality to do so. Players who begin this plan at the age of ten will have the technical abilities of some of the best players by the age of sixteen.

The training program is divided into seven phases, with each one emphasizing specific technical training:

Phase One emphasizes ball contact with specifics on controlling both the ball and the body. This skill is reinforced throughout all the remaining phases.

Phase Two lets the players put the ball techniques of Phase One into practice. Your players learn to keep possession of the ball despite the presence of an opponent, to shield, and to come away with the ball still in your possession.

Phase Three tells how to get past an opponent either alone or with the help of a teammate. Also emphasized is passing; proper use of a pass can cause any defense problems.

Phase Four teaches how to shoot, head, and finish off individual moves. The techniques that are learned are then used in group games in which the emphasis is on scoring.

Phase Five zeroes in on working the techniques that will help you acquire the optimal match condition for your players.

Not until *Phase Six,* when all the attacking techniques have been mastered, is attention given to defense. Only when all the techniques have been learned and applied with speed against full opposition should the sixth phase begin.

Phase Seven emphasizes moving without the ball. The object is to ensure that throughout a game players will be in the right place at the right time.

Naturally, players sixteen and over, for whom competition is important, do not need to adhere precisely to this order. You can vary the phases depending on your team's individual needs and preferences. There are, of course, many more types of practices possible than are offered in this book. You should feel free to improvise and use your creative abilities to elaborate on the various components shown.

The main objective of this training program is to ensure that young players will devote themselves to learning the attacking techniques of the best players. Older players who missed such training in their youth can also use the plan to improve their offensive moves.

The Role of the Coach

To apply this training program to all those who want to become technically creative players, coaches are needed who have mastered its contents and can demonstrate them to perfection. This won't be easy in the beginning, but every player who has command of all the techniques will be eager to pass on that knowledge. Former players are often effective coaches; if you've had to work hard to learn all the moves, it will be easier to convince others of the significance and importance of the exercises.

The head coach ensures that the individual players will receive technical training that is many-sided and creative; the assistant coach turns those individual players into a team. Obviously, the two ideas cannot be entirely separated, because the head coach also works on collective aspects in the training session, while the assistant will do everything possible to make his players better individually, as well as collectively.

When to Start Training

Proper training should begin at ten years of age. If young tennis players, gymnasts, and swimmers can train happily for a few hours each day to improve, so can young soccer players. Coaches must also stress to players the importance of practising outside of team sessions. The result should be direct contact with the ball for a total of at least eight hours a week.

Especially with the youngsters, coaches should always give brief explanations of the exercises, demonstrate them properly, and then correct any errors they observe. There is no point in organizing big games at this stage. Small games will let the players have more ball contact and a chance to try out all the new techniques they have learned. In training sessions, it should be compulsory for players to carry out one of the techniques they have been taught before passing the ball.

During adolescence, even more attention must be paid to coordination when handling the ball. The players must not carry out the exercises in a cramped fashion; the emphasis should always be on flexibility. Now that the players have attained a reasonable proficiency in most techniques, they should start to take the initiative in group games. They should not waste a lot of time and energy simply running around the field. Instead, they should work on as many individual and creative moves as possible.

From the age of thirteen, the training must be not only technically creative but also dynamic and explosive. Up to the age of sixteen players have all the time they need to learn all the techniques and apply them in game situations.

Developing Technique

In the initial training stages, all emphasis should be on technique. Only sprinting speed is inherited; all other skills can be acquired, though it requires years of practice.

Phase One gives rise to the most problems because proper coordination must be learned. This is easier for some players than others. It is critical that players having trouble with coordination be given special help and encouragement as early in training as possible, or they will never get past being technically mediocre players.

Young players often fail to learn from what they see. A single demonstration is not enough to master a new technique; intensive training is needed. If the team sessions are not enough, extra training should be assigned for home. Any player can learn all the techniques, though it will take an older player longer than a younger one—it is easier to learn a new movement than to improve one that you have learned incorrectly. Experience shows that it is easier for a player with a wide range of ball techniques to learn new movements (and enjoy them) than a player with only limited ball-handling skills.

With sufficient practice and repetition, it won't be possible to determine whether a technique is an acquired or a natural movement. This is the point at which a player is ready to try the technique against competition.

Personal and Emotional Growth

Besides technical development, the personal and mental development of players is also crucial. Encourage players to practice the various techniques independently—without waiting for your whistle—and be able to work at developing their own potential.

Players who choose the easiest course in training session by passing the ball to another will do the same

Initial emphasis
is on technique

Anyone can become a good soccer player.

thing in a match. This is *not* what you want your players to do routinely. The techniques learned must be applied. Soccer personalities reveal themselves as such in difficult situations; they make decisive moves.

Tactical Development

If a technically perfect player is weak tactically, he or she will still be helpless in most situations. Choosing the correct tactical solution, making a fast move at the right moment and being in the right position to receive the ball at the right time are not things that can be learned through theory.

Tactical training means looking beyond the ball. Once the techniques are mastered, speed and using the ball to its best advantage are important. Since a player's tactical development does not always match his or her technical expertise, it is up to you as coach to make sure emphasis is placed on both.

Finding That "Something Extra"

Anyone who trains according to this plan knows exactly what he or she is doing. Your players are learning the techniques used by the pros. You won't have players engaged in unrealistic exercises or jumping randomly from one technique to another.

As your players learn the exact purpose for each technique and see the results, they will learn to enjoy practice more and more. You will regularly discuss with your team the group's progress as a whole and individually, and the players will automatically join in the discussion. Healthy development requires that the players do their share of thinking and talking and be capable of self-criticism.

Training requires inspiration and animation. These inner forces determine both how fast a player develops and what level he or she can reach. Make use of your young players' vitality; give them a sufficient taste of success, so that they will become committed to training. All top players have a certain flair, match mentality, self-confidence, and nerve. They have full awareness of what they are doing—and why. They understand that they must always continue to practice and improve.

There is no such animal as the "complete soccer player," any more than there is a "complete coach" or a "complete training program." This training program, however, is proof that any normally gifted player with ambition and the right mentality can learn the techniques of the top soccer players. By learning the techniques in this book, your players will get more pleasure and satisfaction out of playing soccer—and the professional results will bring fans back to the stadiums and fields to cheer on the players of that one-of-a-kind sport—soccer!

Phase One
Controlling the Body and the Ball

Basic techniques

Flexibility and agility on the ball

Fast footwork on the ball

Looking beyond the ball

Feinting while in possession of the ball

Creating and improvising

Kicking technique

The purpose of the first phase is learn as much control as possible er body and ball. It is not the ention to use a host of techniques to monstrate that there is too little ining with the ball in soccer. It uld be easy to fill a whole book erely with exercises on the ball. You ll soon find that out for yourself en you begin intensive training th the ball and discover that you are joying it more and more. Success ts like a stimulant; as soon as you gin to feel you are making progress u want to train even more with the l, thereby increasing your skill. ere is no other sport in which you ed as much technique as in soccer. u are constantly confronted with fferent situations, added to which u have one or more opponents to pe with. Good technique is essen- l for dealing confidently with all e different situations which arise in e course of a game.

The techniques needed for you to come as strong as possible on the ll are divided into five categories,

four of which are dealt with in this first phase. The fifth category, getting past an opponent, is dealt with in phase three. Of the various techniques given here, those that suit a particular player best and prove the most successful will be the ones he will shortly apply in practice.

The emphasis in the second section is on acquiring the necessary flexibility on the ball. The third section is concerned with fast footwork, speeding up the rhythm of the legs. At

the end of each component the player goes through all the exercises mixed up in whatever way he wishes.

The coach must get the players to learn these techniques by constantly repeating each exercise, if necessary through individual training sessions, and they must be given exercises to do as homework, because all of them can be practiced in a small amount of space. Despite the fact that the players have not yet properly mastered the techniques, the training sessions must always be closed or interrupted by a game. This adds to the attractiveness of the sessions. The emphasis in such games must be on the exercises that have been dealt with. The players must be compelled to use the techniques they have learned. As the players are continually dribbling in these sessions this important component does not need to be dealt with. By the time he comes to the end of phase one a player has sufficient control over his body and the ball that he is no longer helpless when he is in possession. He can now go on to develop into a technically skilled, creative player.

1. Basic techniques

Chop the ball across the body with the inside of the right foot, then play it forward with the outside of the left foot. Chop it across the body with the inside of the left foot, and so on.

Chop the ball under the body with the inside of the right instep, play it forward with the inside of the left foot, then repeat.

Chop the ball with the outside of the right foot, play it forward with the inside of the same foot, chop it with the outside of the foot, and so on.

In the same way that a pupil at school cannot progress any further in his studies until he has learned to read and write, a player cannot play or train effectively if he has not mastered the basic techniques. The basic techniques are used in changing direction and swivelling and turning. They also are used in shielding the ball, and controlling and coming away with it when there is no one in a position to

Practicing the basic movements in a zigzag pattern.

11

1. Basic techniques

Chop the ball with the inside of the right instep, play it forward with the outside of the same foot, then chop it with the outside of the foot and play it forward with the inside of the same foot.

Place the outside of the right foot over the ball, turn on your own axis and play the ball with the outside of the foot.

Place the inside of the right foot over the ball, turn on your own axis and play the ball with the inside of the foot.

receive a pass. In situations like this the best players use one or more moves to create an opening or a better situation for a pass. The basic techniques can be practiced in various forms, individually or in twos, in the latter case with one player always resting. They can be practiced in an open space, over the length of the field, zigzag, in a circle, in a triangle,

Practicing the basic movements back and forth.

1. Basic techniques

Play the ball across the body with the toe of the left shoe, then play it forward with the outside of the right foot. Play it back across the body with this foot using the toe of the shoe, etc.

in a square or in free arrangements. As little dribbling as possible is done between the exercises in order to devote as much time and energy as possible to acquiring these techniques. Tempo is adapted to the players' skill.

Turn the ball under the body with the toe of the shoe and play it forward with the inside of the left foot.

Practicing the basic movements at random.

Step over the ball with the inside of the left foot, then play the ball forward with the inside of the right foot. Do the same thing starting with this foot.

1. Basic techniques

Stop the ball, place the same foot over the ball by means of a quick turn and take the ball in the opposite direction.

Trap the ball under the foot, turn quickly and play the ball with the other foot.

Place the leg supporting the weight of the body next to the ball, then play the ball behind the supporting leg with the inside of the other foot.

Practicing the basic movements in turns, zigzag, back and forth, in a small triangle and at random.

1. Basic techniques

Draw the ball towards you under your foot and play it forward again with the outside of the same foot, then do the same thing with the other foot.

Draw the ball back under the foot, stop it with the inside of the same foot and play it forward with the inside of the other foot.

Supporting leg next to the ball, draw the ball under the body and play it across the back of the supporting leg with the inside of the foot.

Practicing the basic movements in threes, with two balls, always with one player resting.

In a circle, working towards a co[ne] and then away from it. All the exe[r]cises can also be carried out in [a] small triangle, zigzag or in a f[ree] arrangement.

Practicing zigzag from cone to co[ne], up on the right, down on the left.

1. Basic techniques

A row of cones, with the players practicing once at a cone and then once in free space, then once at a cone again, etc.

Each player practices the basic techniques in his own triangle.

Practicing zigzag in a circle.

Practicing in threes with two bal.
The two with a ball can practice
they wish and are relieved in turn
the third player.

Practicing in twos with two bal.
back and forth.

1. Basic techniques

Threes with two balls. Two players practice the basic techniques together and are relieved in turn by the player who is resting.

zag arrangement. The player at back works forward, carrying out asic movement when he reaches h player. When he gets to the front takes up position in the zigzag angement.

Twos with one ball in a circle. One the pair rests while the other wor between two players.

Twos with one ball in a circle. One the pair rests while the other wor between the cone in the middle an his partner.

Four pairs working in two triangle In each triangle, two players practi while the other two rest. If the cente cone is taken away, the four pairs ca work around a square.

1. Basic techniques

Twos with one ball in a zigzag arrangement. One rests while the other practices between two players.

These exercises can, of course, also be practiced in a small triangle, back and forth or freely.

Right: Twos in a row. One rests while the other practices between two players.

Twos with one ball. Two players in turn carry out the exercises on each side of the cones.

Above: Fours with two balls. The two with a ball practice on each side of the two resting players. The exercises are always carried out with the outside foot.

Left: Twos with one ball in a square. The exercises can be practiced freely, in a small triangle in front of the player's partner, between two players or around the square.

1. Basic techniques

Twos with one ball in a free arrangement. The players with the balls practice the techniques as they wish.

Twos with one ball in a circle. The one with the ball practices between two players.

Twos with one ball. The players work around the triangle, between two players or freely.

Two groups of three with one b-
each. One player from each gro-
sets off with the ball at speed. Wh-
he reaches the other group he carr-
out a movement and plays the b-
back to his own group. He then jo-
the other group.

Threes with one ball. The player w-
the ball practices between the t-
other players, each player practici-
in turn.

Two groups of three, each with o-
ball. One player from each group s-
off with the ball at speed. When-
reaches the other group he execute-
movement, goes back to the midd-
where he executes another moveme-
then back to the other group aga-
where he executes a third moveme-
before playing the ball back to-
own group and joining the ot-
group.

1. Basic techniques

Three groups of three, each with one ball, in a triangle. One player from each group sets off with the ball at speed towards the next group. When he reaches it he executes a movement, plays the ball back to his own group and joins the group where he is.

Two players at the back set off, execute a movement when they reach the front players, come back, execute another movement when they reach the back players and then take up position at the front.

Below: Threes with one ball. Players take turns to engage in free practice, executing movements when they come to the cones and fellow players.

2. Flexibility and agility on the ball

In carrying out all the basic techniques, concentrate on flexibility and agility. With the inside of the right foot chop the ball to the inside of the left foot, the knees almost touching the ball.

Draw the ball across the body with the toe of the left shoe. Bending the knees deeply, play the ball forward with the outside of the right foot.

Trap the ball with the left foot; move the leg sideways as far as possible and play the ball with the outside of the right foot. Trap the ball with the right foot and repeat.

Scarcely any attention is paid to flexibility and agility on the ball as can be seen from the angular and uneconomical movements characteristic of European players. Players who excel in these things, such as the Brazilians, were born with them; they did not acquire them through special training. The need for special training is evident when you see the woodenness with which young players move. It becomes clear that all those gymnastic exercises do not increase flexibility and agility on the ball. This can only be achieved through appropriate exercises with the ball.

A start has already been made with the basic techniques. These involve total movements in which both the ankle and the hip joints are used, while the spine gets a lot of exercise in all the quick turns that have to be made. All of the basic moves can be used for the purpose of acquiring suppleness and agility on the ball, but the body must now be kept as close to the ground as possible by bending the knees deeply. In changes of direction the supporting leg must be as far away from the ball as possible in order to keep the body low. A player who has flexibility and agility on the ball is more attractive to watch and it costs him less energy to execute moves, whether in training sessions or in a game.

2. Flexibility and agility on the ball

Draw the ball back with the sole of the right shoe, then play it forward with the outside of the same foot.

Practicing the basic techniques individually with the emphasis on flexibility and agility.

Draw the ball back with the sole of the right shoe, then turn it away with the outside of the same foot. Draw the ball back again, etc.

Combination of the previous exercises. Draw the ball back with the sole and play it forward with the outside, draw it back with the sole and turn it away with the outside.

2. Flexibility and agility on the ball

Roll the ball with the inside of the right foot, trap it with the inside of the left foot, tap it and roll it with the inside of the right foot.

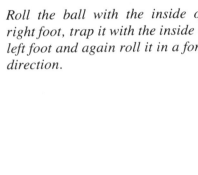

Practicing the basic movements with the emphasis on flexibility and agility.

Roll the ball with the inside of the right foot, trap it with the inside of the left foot and again roll it in a forward direction.

Roll the ball with the outside of the right foot, play it forward with the outside of the left foot, then roll it with the outside of that foot.

2. Flexibility and agility on the ball

Roll the ball under the body with the outside of the left foot, stop the ball with the same foot and roll it with the outside of the other foot.

Practicing the basic techniques in twos with the emphasis on flexibility and agility.

Flick the ball up with the outside of the foot.

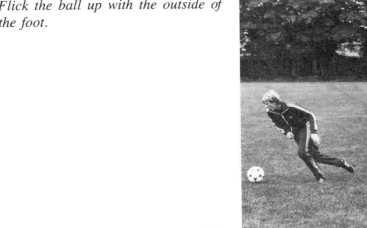

Playing the ball forward with the outside of each foot alternately in a zigzag pattern.

2. Flexibility and agility on the ball

Step over the ball with the inside of the right foot. Play the ball forward with the inside of the left foot and immediately sprint with it. Stop the ball and repeat the exercise in a forward direction.

The same exercise but using the right and left foot alternately, moving back and forth on the same spot.

Practicing in turns in pairs with the emphasis on flexibility and agility.

Step over the ball with the inside of the foot, play it forward with the inside of the other foot while twisting, again step over the ball with the inside of the foot, and so on.

2. Flexibility and agility on the ball

What you see on these pages are merely some examples, because the emphasis is on flexibility and agility in all the forms in which the basic techniques are practiced.

3. Quickness with the feet

Tap the ball under the body from one foot to the other in a zigzag pattern.

Coaches pay little attention to speed of footwork on the ball even though players are given less and less room. The speed with which a player acts when he is in possession is often of decisive importance, particularly in the opposing team's penalty area. These techniques are also needed to dodge tackles by defenders. Again, use can be made here of the basic techniques, but now the contact of the feet with the ball must be as fast and supple as possible. After each exercise the ball is tapped quickly to the other foot and the exercise repeated with this foot. This means that a player touches the ball thousands of times an hour, which in addition to improving his rhythm of movement and speed of footwork also develops the feel for the ball in both legs. All players greatly enjoy these exercises, which can be carried out in a small amount of space.

Chop the ball with the inside of the left instep to the inside of the right foot. Give it a couple of quick taps and chop it with the inside of the instep of the right foot.

Play the ball under the body to the inside of the left foot with the toe of the shoe. Give it a couple of quick taps and then play it under the body with the toe of the right foot.

3. Quickness with the feet

Roll the ball under the right foot, give it a couple of taps and roll it under the left foot.

Tap the ball with the bottom of the left foot to the inside of the right foot, give it a couple of intermediate taps, then tap it back with the bottom of the foot to the inside of the left foot.

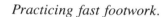

Practicing fast footwork.

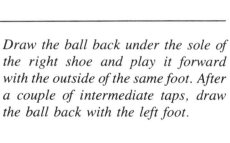

Draw the ball back under the sole of the right shoe and play it forward with the outside of the same foot. After a couple of intermediate taps, draw the ball back with the left foot.

3. Quickness with the feet

Draw the ball back to the inside of the left foot, tap it a couple of times and then draw it back with the right foot to the inside of that foot.

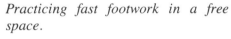

Practicing fast footwork in a free space.

Draw the ball back under the right shoe and play it forward or sideways with the outside of the same foot. Give it a couple of taps and repeat with the left foot.

Roll the outside of the right foot over the ball and play it with the inside to the inside of the left foot. Give it a couple of taps and repeat with the other foot.

3. Quickness with the feet

Place the left foot on the ball, make a quick turn, take the ball over with the right foot and play it forward with the inside of this foot. Give it a couple of taps and repeat the exercise starting with the right foot.

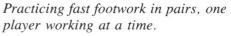

Practicing fast footwork in pairs, one player working at a time.

Roll the ball back and forth under the right foot, tap it a couple of times and roll it back and forth under the left foot.

Roll the ball away with the outside of the left foot and with the inside of the same foot play it to the inside of the right foot. Give it a couple of taps and repeat starting with the right foot.

3. Quickness with the feet

Draw the ball back and play it with the inside of the right foot to the inside of the left foot. Give it a couple of taps and do the same thing starting with the left foot. You practice in one place.

Place the left foot on the ball. As you are making a quick turn, take the ball over with the right foot and play it forward with the outside of the foot. Give it a couple of taps and repeat starting with the right foot.

Draw the ball back with the left toe, then draw it back with the inside of the right foot and play it forward with the outside of the instep of that foot. Give it a couple of taps and repeat starting with the right foot.

Practicing fast footwork in threes, with one player always resting.

3. Quickness with the feet

What you see on these pages are merely some examples, because the emphasis is on speed of footwork in all the forms in which the basic techniques are practiced.

4. Looking beyond the ball

Players with technical limitations can never make fast plays because, even where there is no opponent, all their attention is on the ball and they cannot survey the field. For this reason there is no point in technically limited players engaging in group games or combination forms in which the ball can be touched only once or twice. No coach needs to tell a soccer star what to do in unpredictable match situations.

These players take in the situation even before they have possession of the ball. They scarcely pay any attention to the ball, yet they have it under control. This section provides a basis for achieving this by having players carry out all the techniques in the previous sections but looking as much as possible beyond the ball. This will be required of the players throughout the rest of the program.

As soon as the players have mastered all the ball techniques they must practice carrying them out while looking beyond the ball.

5. Feinting while in possession of the ball

Place the right foot next to the ball. The moment the heel is alongside it, hit the ball with the inside of the foot against the inside of the left foot.

Pretend to be about to kick the ball but at the last moment take it forward with the outside of the kicking foot.

Pretend to be about to kick but at the last moment chop the ball under your body to the inside of the other foot.

The different ways of catching an opponent on the wrong foot by feinting are too numerous to be included in one book. However, feinting is also used to win possession of the ball and to put off balance an opponent who has the ball. Unfortunately, teams consist almost exclusively of players who seldom, if ever, feint. This has made soccer more predictable and, hence, less interesting. A player who wants to be able to get past his man must know the basic techniques, but he must also learn how to feint. This should not be any problem once you have mastered the basic movements, because many of them are used in feinting as well as in other components of the game. You will see for yourself that any opponent reacts to a feint. Shortly you will be required to put as many feints as possible into practice. In time you will automatically begin to use the types of feints that suit you best and it will no longer even be possible to tell whether they are natural or acquired.

5. Feinting while in possession of the ball

Pretend to be about to kick but tap the ball behind the supporting leg and take it away.

Practicing feinting.

Step over the ball then play it forward with the inside of the other foot.

Pretend to be breaking into a run but come back to the starting position.

5. Feinting while in possession of the ball

Pretend to be passing the ball but carry it along with the inside of the right foot and take it over with the outside of the left foot.

Pretend to be about to kick but at the last moment trap the ball, shield it with your body and take it away with the other foot.

Pairs with two balls practicing feinting.

Pretend to be about to kick the ball but take it away with the outside of the foot.

5. Feinting while in possession of the ball

Pretend to backheel the ball but accelerate in a forward direction.

Draw the ball back, then carry it forward with the outside of the instep of the same foot.

Practicing feinting kicks.

Pretend to be about to play the ball with the inside of the foot. The foot stops on top of the ball and you turn it behind the supporting leg.

5. Feinting while in possession of the ball

You pretend to chop the ball inwards but put your foot behind it and flick it over the opponent's leg.

Pretend to be about to kick the ball with the inside of the foot, but roll the foot over the ball and draw it back.

Practicing feinting with an opponent.

Pretend to be about to kick but turn the ball under the body with the toe and carry it away in the opposite direction.

All the feints can be executed in the practice forms used for the basic techniques. As soon as players have mastered them individually they are practiced against an opponent.

Practicing feinting a kick.

5. Feinting while in possession of the ball

Players practicing feints. Fixed pairs of players, each with a ball, practice the movements opposite one another in a free space. Then opponents take up positions and the players in possession practice against them at random.

5. Feinting while in possession of the ball

Players practicing feints in the presence of an opponent.

Four players with two balls. The two players in possession make a feint and move sideways. The defenders keep on turning to face their new opponent.

6. Creating and improvising

Roll the ball with the inside of the right foot against the left foot, then draw the ball back and again roll it.

Draw the ball back and play it forward with the outside of the foot, then step over it and play it forward again.

Trap the ball, place the right foot beyond the ball; you pretend that you are going to play the ball forward with the outside of the right foot but play it with the outside of the left foot.

These are merely three examples. The number of possibilities is infinite. All of the ball techniques can be put to use.

When you have learned to execute all the techniques perfectly at speed, it is no longer necessary to practice them individually. The most important quality needed by a player is the ability to create and improvise. In no other sport does a player with the ball have so much scope to give free rein to his creative capacities. In training a player, therefore, creative and improvisational ability must be worked on right from the start. The game is crying out for players with fully developed creative capabilities. In this section, all the techniques must be practiced in any combinations the player wishes.

Regardless of age or ability level, the players can indulge themselves to the full. In doing so they will discover ever more possibilities and moves with the ball, and the stimulus this provides will make them work at it all the harder. You must make sure, however, that the moves are not carried out in a monotonous tempo. Players must work with changes of rhythm.

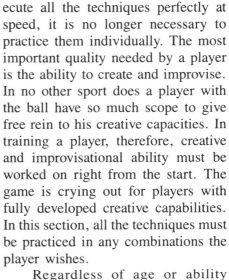

Practicing creative and improvisational ability is the best individua[l] training and it can also be don[e] outside the official sessions as homework. Naturally, a player must also b[e] able to create and improve agains[t] opposition, which is why defender[s] are brought in.

6. Creating and improvising

The two players with the soccer balls must try to lift them over the defender into the goal. At a later stage the defender can try to head the balls away from the goal.

Working in pairs, the players pu curving shots into the adjacent goal

7. Kicking technique

The pairs of players with the soccer balls must try to lift them diagonally over the defenders into the adjacent goal.

The pair with the balls center curving shots; the other two put them in past the near post. When all the balls have been used, the pairs switch jobs.

Kicking technique cannot be practiced effectively until the players have gone through the exercises in the previous sections. Kicking and trapping are above all a question of feel for the ball. This explains why all technically gifted players have a good kicking technique even though they have undergone no special training for it. Having a feel for the ball also makes it a lot easier to develop the player's weak leg, something which must be done. In modern soccer players have neither the time nor the space to transfer the ball to their strong leg.

Kicking practice can take a varied form, with the coach determining distance and intensity. In practicing kicking techniques you automatically practice trapping. As kicking technique also forms part of the sections on receiving and coming away with the ball, getting past an opponent, making one-two combinations, shooting and heading, every player should acquire a good kicking technique without any trouble.

Six players form a circle. The two players in possession dribble the ball to the middle and play it on the turn to the next player.

Left: The players at the back pass deep diagonal balls. The players in the middle go for them, control them and make deep diagonal passes back.

7. Kicking technique

The player at the back lifts the ball over the head of the player in the middle; the front man plays it with one touch to the middle man, who takes it and changes places with the front man. The front man then lifts the ball over the middle man to the player at the back.

Six players form a circle. They are divided into two groups of three. Each group has two balls. As a player passes one ball, the other is on its way to him.

The player at the back lifts the ba[ll] over the head of the middle player an[d] gets it back immediately. Then h[e] moves to the front where he receive[s] the ball from the man who is now [at] the back.

The same exercise is repeated wit[h] four players and four balls, down th[e] length of the field.

The outside men play the balls to th[e] inside men, who take them and pla[y] them back. The inside players the[n] turn to receive the next balls from th[e] other outside players.

7. Kicking technique

Two men face each other and each kicks a soccer ball simultaneously to the other player.

Two pairs, overlapping, each player with a ball. The members of each pair kick the balls simultaneously over the heads of the members of the other pair who are standing between them.

Three players form a large triangle. A fourth player has the ball, which he kicks past one of the players on the inside while he sprints around him on the outside. He then passes the ball to that player and takes his place in the triangle. The player who now has the ball does the same thing with the next player in the triangle.

Three men, two balls. The man at the front plays the ball to the middle man, who receives it and takes up position next to the front man. The front man, meanwhile, receives the second ball from the player at the back.

Two groups of three, each group with one ball. The players with the balls pass them to the other players in their group. The players receiving the balls take their place and move sideways into the other group.

7. Kicking technique

Six players in a circle, two balls. Each player with a ball passes it to the second player from him in the circle, who passes it back to the player who has been skipped. The players continue passing around the circle in this alternating pattern.

The players with the balls kick them to their partners, who try to trap them in any way they can. When all the balls have been used up the partners switch jobs.

Phase Two
Dominating the Opponent

. *Receiving the ball and moving
with it*

. *Shielding the ball*

. *Dribbling to beat an opponent*

. *Group games (scrimmages)*

Now that you have discovered in ⱡe first phase that you can be sucⱡessful with the ball, you will have ⱡore of the inner stimulation required ⱡr your further development as a ⱡayer. No doubt you have gained so ⱡuch self-confidence that you are ⱡying to use all the moves you have ⱡarned to dominate an opponent. ⱡhis is where the emphasis lies in the ⱡcond phase. Ball possession must ⱡw be put to the best possible use—

baffling your opponents. In this phase independence, flair and self-confidence are required. Colorless soccer is no longer acceptable; all of the moves must be used to outplay your opponent. And the amount of resistance offered by that opponent will gradually be increased.

In the course of the exercises and games a player must practice all the ball techniques in order to discover which of them are best suited to a given situation in his case and with which of them he achieves most success.

The situation is determined now by the player with the ball, whose job it is to outplay his opponent.

Two players kick the balls diagonall[y] and change places with the player[s] who have received them.

The outside players pass the balls to the inside players, who take them on the turn and pass them to the opposite outside players.

1. Receiving the ball and moving with it

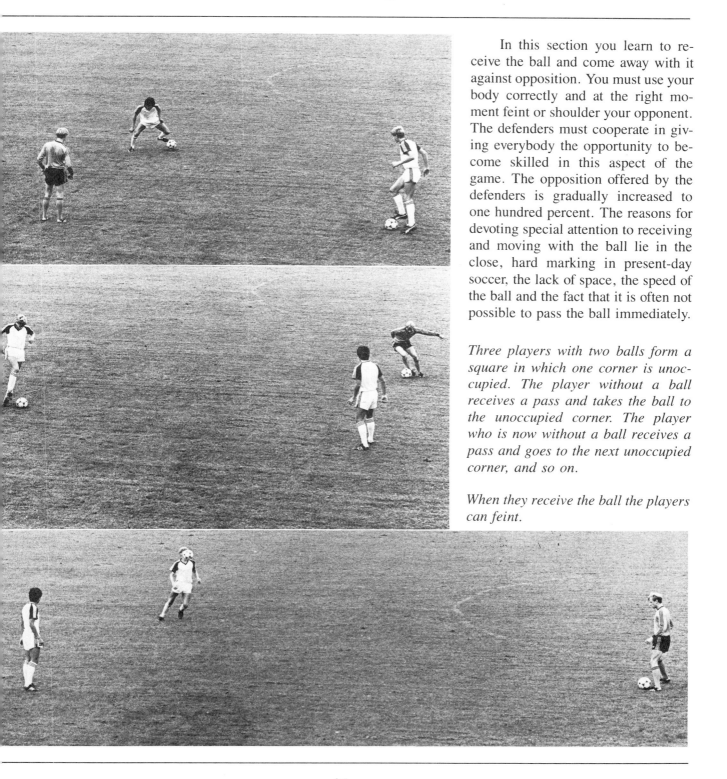

In this section you learn to receive the ball and come away with it against opposition. You must use your body correctly and at the right moment feint or shoulder your opponent. The defenders must cooperate in giving everybody the opportunity to become skilled in this aspect of the game. The opposition offered by the defenders is gradually increased to one hundred percent. The reasons for devoting special attention to receiving and moving with the ball lie in the close, hard marking in present-day soccer, the lack of space, the speed of the ball and the fact that it is often not possible to pass the ball immediately.

Three players with two balls form a square in which one corner is unoccupied. The player without a ball receives a pass and takes the ball to the unoccupied corner. The player who is now without a ball receives a pass and goes to the next unoccupied corner, and so on.

When they receive the ball the players can feint.

Each pair in the middle competes for a ball passed in from the two outside players. The winner in each pair passes the ball back to the outside player and changes places with him.

The outside men who put the ball into play go to the middle and form new pairs with the losers and the drill is repeated.

1. Receiving the ball and moving with it

The winner of the duel comes away with the ball, then backheels it to the loser and joins the third player to form a new pair. The loser then plays the ball to them and the duel drill is repeated.

The winner of the duel takes the ball to the place where it was put into play, thus forming a new pair. The loser plays the ball to the other pair.

The winners of the duels play the ball diagonally to the losers, then join the solo players to form new pairs. The losers then play the balls to the new pairs.

1. Receiving the ball and moving with it

The pairs in the middle compete for the balls. The winners take the balls in a backward direction, pass them to the outside players and take their places.

The winner moves back with the ball. The man who has played it to the pair joins the loser and the winner then plays to the ball to them.

The player interposes his body between the ball and his opponent at the right moment, making use of the basic techniques.

The players in possession shield the ball, using whichever basic movement they choose.

2. Shielding the ball

Good players always place their body between the ball and the opponent at the right moment, not only to shield the ball but also to permit a quick resumption of play. As all the basic techniques can be used in doing this, it can be practiced in a highly varied way.

You can use both legs, which is a great advantage, while looking beyond the ball. Suppleness and agility are also important. The exercises are enjoyable to do, with the player daring his opponent to come for the ball and then interposing his body at the right moment.

Naturally, when you come to apply what you have learned in match situations you will automatically use the techniques that suit you best.

Shielding the ball in a free space.

Left: The defenders and the players in possession move freely among the group, with the players in possession continually placing their body between the ball and a defender at the right moment.

Right: Pairs with one ball. The player in possession repeatedly goes to the defender and shields the ball by means of a basic movement.

Pairs arranged in a circle. The players in possession work back and forth between two defenders.

2. Shielding the ball

The players in possession take turns in approaching the defender. As soon as he goes for the ball they shield it and take up position again.

Left: Pairs practicing shielding the ball in turns.

Groups of four with two balls. The outside players act as defenders. The players in possession work back and forth, constantly keeping their body between the ball and the defenders.

Three players arrange themselves in square with one unoccupied corne The two players in possession tak turns in moving to the unoccupie corner, but there they encounter th defender. They shield the ball and g back to their own corner.

Shielding the ball against ful opposition.

2. Shielding the ball

Three pairs, each with one ball, arrange themselves in a triangle. The players in possession work around the triangle, shielding the ball with a basic movement when they come to a defender.

Two pairs, each with one ball. The players in possession work back and forth, the other two players acting as defenders.

Same setup, but now you make for the unoccupied corner after the ball has been passed to you.

The player in possession darts explosively past the defender.

Three players with two balls in a square with one unoccupied corner. The players in possession set off in turns for the unoccupied corner, where they encounter a defender. They beat the defender by means of a basic technique and take his place.

3. Dribbling to beat an opponent

The ability to shake off opponents by dribbling is one of the most important attributes needed by a player if he is to play competitive soccer. It is difficult to reach players with long passes and as soon as you try to run with the ball you encounter an opponent. In situations like this most players avoid taking any risks by passing the ball on to a teammate or kick it upfield at random, which usually results in loss of possession.

If dull uniformity is to be avoided, it is essential that this aspect of the game should be practiced with courage and without the fear of failure. What has been learned about shielding the ball can be put to good use here, as can all the basic techniques and feints. As soon as you have beaten your direct opponent you move upfield with the ball at your feet. The best possible use must be made of ball possession every time. In this section the players must continually dribble the ball free, shield it, and move up with it applying basic techniques and feinting techniques. If these things are not repeated endlessly in practice they will never be used in a game.

After the player in possession has beaten his opponent he passes the ball to the neutral player, who has meanwhile passed his ball to the defender. He in turn tries to beat the defender who is coming for him.

The player in possession tries to dribble the ball over the line, while the defender tries to stop him.

Two attackers take turns in trying to dribble the ball over the line, which is guarded by a single defender.

Three attackers and three defenders engage in one-on-one duels in turns.

As soon as an attacker loses the ball he becomes a defender.

3. Dribbling to beat an opponent

Two groups of three, facing one another. The players in possession use a basic technique to beat the defenders as they come in. They switch roles and repeat the drill.

Two groups of three. The players in possession force back the defenders, who offer graduated amounts of resistance. The players switch roles, and repeat.

Two pairs play one against one in a demarcated area. The players can score by dribbling the ball over the imaginary line. After a while the players in the middle change places with the other four.

Two pairs play one against one in a demarcated area. As soon as a player loses the ball he drops out to rest. The waiting player comes in fresh and takes the role of defender. The previous defender takes on the role of attacker.

3. Dribbling to beat an opponent

One against one in a demarcated area. The winners always play against one another.

Three pairs play one against one in a demarcated area. Players can score by dribbling the ball over the imaginary line.

Three pairs play one against one in a demarcated area.

Two against two with one neutral player in a demarcated area. Players can score by dribbling the ball over the imaginary line.

Two against two in a demarcated area. Players can score by dribbling the ball over the imaginary line. The player who scores retains possession.

One against one in a demarcated area with two neutral assistants. The neutral assistants stay on the touchline or boundary line and one-touch the ball back onto the field to the same player. The players in the middle must make as many individual moves as possible and can score by dribbling the ball over the imaginary line. The player in possession may make use of the services of the assistants for passing purposes, while the assistants may also pass to each other. After a given number of plays, the two in the middle change places with the two assistants. (Assistants must only one-touch all passes.)

4. Group games (scrimmages)

Three against three. The player in possession uses basic and feinting techniques. Players can score by dribbling the ball over the imaginary line.

Right: Two against two with two neutral assistants now in the field of play in a demarcated rea. Players in possession must make as many individual moves as possible. The assistants are allowed to pass to one another. There is continuous switching of roles.

Now that the players have developed skill with the ball as well as without an opponent they can start playing games. The numbers in the games must be kept small in order to ensure that players are in possession of the ball as often as possible. The emphasis in the games is on individual moves. Players who perform monotonously and simply pass the ball on to teammates without trying anything themselves are benched. This is repeated until such time as they come to realize that they will never become good players by passing the ball on whenever they get it. All their energy and positive aggressiveness must be put into individual play.

Only when you are capable of undertaking something on your own can you develop into a soccer personality. It does not matter if individual moves lead to loss of possession in the beginning. This is still where the emphasis must be placed.

The players now possess sufficient technical and creative qualities that to have possession of the ball and not use it is a waste.

The defenders must save as much of their strength as they can by making their opposition as flexible as possible. In time the players will auto-

Four against two. The player in possession has to touch the ball at least three times before passing. If he loses possession he switches with the defender.

103

One against one with four neutral one-touch line assistants on the touch lines who must one-touch pass.

Two pairs play one-on-one with four neutral assistants. Players can score by dribbling the ball over the imaginary line.

Two against two with one neutral player. Players can score by passing the ball to their partner between two cones.

4. Group games (scrimmages)

Two against two with four neutral assistants. Alternate the roles.

matically discover which techniques are most successful. Meanwhile their capacity for observing and reacting and their timing will be developed without effort.

Three against three with the emphasis on individual play when in possesion. Players can score by passing the ball to one of their teammates between the two cones.

One against one with one neutral player and two neutral assistants. The neutral player and the assistants are only allowed to touch the ball once. The two players must engage in as much individual play as possible. They can score by dribbling the ball over the imaginary line.

Phase Three
Beating and Bypassing Opponents

1. *Techniques for beating opponents*
2. *Practicing the techniques under pressure*
3. *Beating an opponent or a one-two combination*
4. *Passing to an upcoming player*
5. *Group games (scrimmages)*

In the first phase you devoted all your energy to becoming as skillful and as many-sided as possible when in possession of the ball. In the second phase these techniques were used to outplay an opponent. By now certain techniques are working better than others and inner stimulation and inspiration will play an increasingly important part in your further development. You feel more self-confident with the ball and you want to do

more. In this phase you must have the self-confidence and flair needed to beat your man or bypass him by means of a one-two combination.

The fact that you now have mastery over your body and the ball means that you can also master your opponent. In this phase you have the opportunity to get past an opponent by dribbling or using a one-two combination. Make use of it. This does not apply only to attackers, because the ability to get past an opponent is also extremely important in a midfielder or a defender. Without this ability you will always be a limited player, unable to create chances or maneuver teammates into the kinds of positions that produce goals. Only top players force openings through individual play. Without such individual capacities they would be helpless, no different from all the average players. Most players are not even capable of getting past an opponent even with someone to help them. When they are faced with a superior defensive force in the penalty area they are completely impotent. Even highly expensive attackers are neutralized without any trouble by a personal marker if they don't receive any help in the form of teammates able to run onto a pass placed behind the defenders.

All too often you see a defender pass the ball to a forward with a marker behind him. That is one possibility, but the situation becomes much more interesting if the defender can beat his opponent and then combine his creative abilities with those of the forward to shake off the latter's marker. Simply getting rid of the ball

to a teammate has never yet produced an exciting situation in a game of soccer.

1. Techniques for beating an opponent

With spring in your supporting left leg, draw the ball towards you with the inside of the right foot, then take it away explosively with the outside of that foot.

The same exercise except that you use the outside of the foot to flick the ball over the imaginary leg of an opponent.

Again the same exercise, but instead of playing the ball with the outside of the right foot, you step sideways and take the ball away with the outside of the left foot.

You scarcely ever see a player beat an opponent on his own nowadays, even though it is precisely things like this that the public come to see. Even worse, you never see players practicing the techniques for beating an opponent, which means that the coaches either do not have command of the techniques or don't consider them important. Personally, I'm more inclined to believe the former. I see coaches become indignant when a player loses the ball trying to get past an opponent, but nothing at all is said about players who simply get rid of the ball, or about players who lose the ball through bad passing. Many coaches even go so far as to forbid gifted players to beat their man on their own. If the great soccer personalities of the past had been treated in the same way they would never have emerged from the ranks of the nondescript.

Any normally gifted player can learn every technique for beating a man. And they can be learned all the easier after the improvement in coordination achieved in the preceding phases. Another advantage is that the basic techniques and feints from the previous phases can now be used for getting past an opponent. As with all techniques, the techniques for beating a man are practiced as often as possible, until they have been perfectly mastered. The amount of resistance offered by the opponent is then gradually increased. Finally, all of the techniques are used in a variety of group games against full opposition. This will enable you to discover for yourself which techniques are best suited

1. Techniques for beating an opponent

The scissors. Step over the ball with your left foot and take the ball away explosively with the outside of the right foot.

to you. Once you achieve success with particular techniques you continue to use them. When you have finally mastered the art of beating your opponent at the right moment you will be worth more to your team than ten ball-passers together.

The same exercise except that now you step over the ball with your right foot and take it away with the outside of your left.

Double scissors. Step over the ball quickly with your left foot, then with your right and take it away explosively with the outside of your left foot.

The player in possession of the ball beats his opponent, then passes to the third player, who in turn beats him and passes to the other player.

1. Techniques for beating an opponent

The scissors around the ball. Step around the ball with your right foot and take the ball away with the outside of your left foot.

Pretend to be going past your opponent to the right, then take the ball away explosively with the outside of your left foot.

The player in possession beats his opponent, then stops the ball and switches to the role of defender.

Step sideways over the ball with your left foot, then take it away with the outside of your right foot.

1. Techniques for beating an opponent

You pretend to be about to chop the ball inwards with your right foot but take it away explosively with the outside of the right foot.

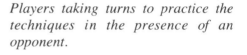

Players taking turns to practice the techniques in the presence of an opponent.

Pretend to be about to chop the ball with your left foot, but take it away with your right.

You pretend to be going to the right by tapping the ball with the inside of your left foot to the inside of your right, then set off in the opposite direction.

1. Techniques for beating an opponent

Pretend to be about to play the ball past your opponent with your right foot, then draw the ball across your body and take it past him with the inside of the other foot.

The defenders try to dispossess the attackers.

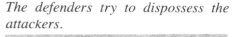

Pretend to be about to chop the ball with your right foot, but move your foot to the side of the ball and take it away with the outside of your left foot.

Take a long step over the ball with your left leg, thus shielding it from your opponent, then turn it away from him using the outside of your right foot.

Practicing the techniques for beating an opponent in a zigzag pattern, back and forth.

Two groups of players, each play with a ball. Two players practice the techniques, then go to the back of the line.

2. Practicing the techniques under pressure

The scissors, with the player playing the ball past his opponent with the outside of his right foot.

With spring in your left supporting leg, draw the ball towards you with the inside of the right foot, then play it quickly past your opponent with the outside of the foot.

All the techniques must be practiced with an opponent. The player in possession of the ball steps over the ball with his right foot and then takes it away with the instep of his left foot, which places his body between the ball and his opponent.

The players beat their opponent then play the ball back and become defenders.

Each of the players has a ball and they take turns in beating one another.

Four players with two balls arrange themselves in a triangle. The player in possession beats an opponent, who then receives the other ball and beats the next player.

2. Practicing the techniques under pressure

Threes with one ball. The player in possession beats his opponent and passes the ball to the third player, whom he then challenges in the role of defender.

The middle player receives the ball, turns with it and beats the third player. He then passes it to the third player, who turns with it and beats the first.

Threes with two balls. Two players practice the techniques for beating an opponent. The first one faces the third player then passes his ball to him, whereupon the third player joins the second player (in the middle) with a ball, who has turned to face him.

The same setup, but now the player tap the ball past their opponent on one side and run around him on the other.

Four players form a square. Two of them receive balls from two defenders, whom they then beat. Having done this they pass the balls to the next players and become defenders.

Threes with two balls. The player in possession who is nearest the man without a ball beats him. The defender then receives the other ball and becomes the attacker.

2. Practicing the techniques under pressure

...rees with two balls. The players in possession take turns in beating the ...fender. A player who fails to beat him becomes the defender.

Four players in possession beat two defenders, one after the other. Players who fail become defenders.

...ur players in possession beat two defenders in turn. Players who fail become ...fenders.

Three players, one of whom receives a ball from a fourth player, beats h[is] opponent and passes the ball back to the fourth player. The defender h[as] meanwhile received a ball from the fourth player and beats the man facing hi[m].

When he has been beaten, the defender receives a ball from the man at the back and beats the player in front of him.

Two players in possession try to beat two defenders and dribble the ball ov[er] the line. The other two players with balls then pass them to the defenders, w[ho] try to dribble them over the other line.

2. Practicing the techniques under pressure

...ree players with two balls take it in ...rns to beat an opponent standing in ...e middle. The ball is then lobbed ...ck to the waiting player.

Two players in possession and one defender. The two in possession take it in turns to beat the defender by flicking the ball over his right leg, then left leg.

...ree players in possession take turns ...trying to beat a defender. A player ...ho fails becomes the defender.

The player in possession beats the defender by dribbling or with a one-two combination. After a given number of plays the three switch roles.

Two defenders, two one-touch assistants and three players who take turns in beating the defenders by dribbling or with a one-two combination. A player who loses possession becomes a defender.

3. Beating an opponent or a one-two combination

The player in possession gets past his opponent with a one-two combination. He then passes the ball to his partner in the combination, who beats him by dribbling or making a one-two combination with the third player.

The player in possession tries to beat his opponent as often as possible by dribbling or making a one-two combination. When he loses possession the players switch roles.

Beating an opponent becomes really easy when a teammate presents himself at the right moment for a one-two combination. After dribbling, the best way of getting past one or more opponents is a one-two combination. Unfortunately, successful one-two combinations are also becoming an increasingly rare sight. The reasons for this lie in tough man-to-man marking, the speed of play and lack of space, and also in the players' limited technical abilities.

Coaches must come to realize that all their practicing against cones and passive opponents is completely pointless. A successful one-two combination requires two players with soccer intelligence and a feel for the ball, neither of which you can acquire by practicing one-two combinations

The three players in white shirts take turns in beating the second defender by dribbling or making a one-two combination. They then beat the first defender, with the second defender assisting in the one-two combinations.

Three players in warm-up suits w
two balls take turns in beating th
opponent by dribbling or making or
two combinations with one of the t
one-touch assistants in white shir.
When the defender is beaten he r
ceives the other ball and becomes t
attacker.

Left: The ball is passed to the mark
player, who returns it with one touc
The first player then either beats t
marker by dribbling or plays a de
pass to his sprinting partner.

3. Beating an opponent or a one-two combination

The player in the foreground lobs the ball to his partner and positions himself for a one-two combination. The player in the background then lobs the ball and positions himself for a one-two combination. A player who loses the ball becomes the defender.

Below: Three players, each with a ball, take turns in beating the defender by dribbling or making a one-two combination. A player who loses the ball becomes the defender.

against a cone. The second player must have various options, and in many cases he will have to pass to someone else. This is practiced particularly in the group games at the end of this section.

Once you have mastered the techniques for beating a man and have also acquired the soccer intelligence and feel for the ball required for a perfect one-two combination, you will have no need to fear any defender. In the different group games

The player in possession beats his opponent and passes to the third player. The neutral, or one-touch, assistant is available for one-two combinations.

Player makes a one-two combination with the furthest player, who then receives a lob from the other side and makes either a long or a short one-two combination.

Five players, two of them in the middle. The first player in the middle receives the ball and hits it back the first time. The second player is beaten either by dribbling or by a one-two combination.

3. Beating an opponent or a one-two combination

and competitive forms of practice, the defenders must do everything possible to intercept the ball. If they succeed, they are rewarded with possession and it is then their turn to try to get past the opponents. In practicing one-two combinations the value of being able to look beyond the ball will become evident.

Repeated one-two combinations, with the players in the middle alternately acting as defender and wall passer for the combinations.

The player in dark shorts gets past his opponent either by beating him or with a one-two combination and takes up position beyond the defender. The other defender then plays the ball to the other player in dark shorts, who in turn gets past his opponent either by beating him or with a one-two combination and takes up position beyond him.

Two players get past the defender by means of a one-two combination. The defender then receives the ball from the player in the foreground and beats him. The defender receives the ball from the other end and chooses between beating his man and a one-two combination.

Three players take turns in getting past a defender by beating him or making use of a long one-two combination. A player who loses the ball becomes the defender.

Two defenders try to prevent the attackers, in white shirts, from crossing the imaginary line by beating their man or making a one-two combination with the player behind the line. The players in the dark shorts then pass their balls to the defenders, who become the attackers and try to do the same thing.

The player in the foregound lofts the ball over the defender. He takes up position and the player with the ball gets past the defender either by beating him or by making use of a one-two combination. The first player then takes up position next to the defender, who receives the ball from the player at the back.

3. Beating an opponent or a one-two combination

The player at the back must get past the two defenders, in the light shirts, by dribbling or by means of a short or long one-two combination.

Three players take turns in trying to get past two defenders, either by dribbling or by means of a short or long one-two combination.

The player in possession beats his opponent or passes to the player coming up in support. The defender then receives the other ball and the player behind him without a ball acts as the supporting player.

Left: Three pairs, each with a ball. The player without a ball takes up position as a defender; once he has performed his task as a defender, his partner, who is behind him with a ball, sets off and he becomes the supporting player.

Pairs take turns in trying to get past a defender by beating him or playing a through pass to the player coming up in support.

4. Passing to an upcoming player

Players running between or around defenders to take a through pass are almost unstoppable provided the timing is right. The defenders have their backs to the goal and are concentrating on the player with the ball. This means that players who are coming through quickly to take a good pass are extremely difficult to deal with despite the presence of a sweeper. There is always panic of some kind in the defense and the positional changes that take place create new openings. It is an ideal weapon, yet one that is far too seldom used.

As with almost all the other components, you can practice this in a variety of group games and competitive forms of training until strikers and midfielders can be certain that supporting players will be sprinting past them as soon as they get possession of the ball.

A player who makes too little use of this dangerous weapon must be made the neutral player, which means that he will be continually sprinting past the man in possession to defeat one defender after another.

Three pairs take turns in trying to get past each other using dribbling and passes to the supporting player.

Two against two, the aim being to dribble the ball over the line. The neutral player acts as a supporting player, coming up to take through passes from whichever side is in possession.

Two pairs. With the help of a neutral player, the pair in possession try to get past their opponents as often as possible by dribbling and passing to players coming up in support.

One against one, with two neutral one-touch line assistants. The players must beat their man and make one-two combinations as often as possible. The game can also be played with the object of dribbling the ball over the line. Players and assistants repeatedly switch roles.

Two against two with one neutral player. A team gets one point every time they get past their opponents by dribbling or a successful one-two combination. The game is then played with the object of dribbling the ball over the line, with the scoring team remaining in possession.

One against one with four neutral one-touch assistants on the touch line. If the players in the middle cannot receive a pass the assistants can pass to one another.

5. Group games (scrimmages)

Two against two, with two one-touch assistants, with as much dribbling and as many one-two combinations as possible.

At the end of the second phase, every time they were in possession players had to apply the techniques they had learned to get past their opponent. Every opportunity provided by possession must now be used to beat one or more opponents. In doing so players will automatically improve their mastery of the techniques that have been acquired so far.

Lack of independence and personality are not accepted. You have to realize that you must become somebody as a player, otherwise you will

Two pairs play one against one, with four neutral one-touch assistants on the touch lines. The players in the middle must exercise their creative capacities to the fullest.

Four against two. The four must make as many one-two combinations as possible.

not achieve the principal objective of this training plan. When you are in possession of the ball unchallenged, rather than simply getting rid of it to a teammate, you must take the ball to an opponent and try to beat him in whatever way you choose. You can indulge your creative powers even more than in the earlier games. In doing this you will improve your grasp of the game, your powers of observation and your ability to react. Particularly suitable here are games with one or more assistants, because

*Two against two, with four one-touc[h]
line assistants.*

*Left: Three pairs, with two assistant[s].
The first pair try to dribble the ba[ll]
over the line. The ball is then playe[d]
to the defenders, who try to dribbl[e]
the ball over the line defended by th[e]
third pair.*

*Two against two, with four assistant[s]
who can operate over the entire lin[e]
between the cones. If there is n[o]
player in a position to receive a pas[s]
the assistants* can pass to each other[.]

5. Group games (scrimmages)

Top: Three against three, with two assistants. The aim is to dribble the ball as often as possible over the opponents' line. A team which does so retains possession of the ball.

Three against three, with three one-touch assistants, the assistants repeatedly changing places with one of the teams. The object is for players to exercise their creative powers to the fullest.

Three groups of three. Two teams play against each other. Two members of the third group act as assistants; the third is a neutral player and supports the team in possession. The aim is for the teams to dribble the ball over the line as often as possible, using their creative powers to the fullest. A team which scores retains possession.

they make the games more stimulating for the players and permit substitutions to be made when players tire. When you play a game with one, two, three or four assistants you gradually begin to feel that you are becoming somebody as a player. The days when you were merely a ball-passer have gone forever. You now have command of all the techniques needed to get past defenders and by making full use of them you improve your grasp of the game, with the result that you become increasingly important to your team.

Phase Four
Creating Chances and Using Them

. Shooting

. Heading

. Individual play

. Group games (scrimmages)

Now we come to the finishing touches. Only when you have mastered all the techniques can you create chances without resorting to kick-and-run soccer. Players train daily in the goal area, yet in matches you seldom see chances created by means of attacking techniques. Most players do not have them at their command, even though they have to deal with a wall of defenders in top condition. The first three phases were necessary in order to acquire the mastery of attacking techniques needed to create chances.

A player who has acquired these important techniques will not only have the will to get to the goal; he will also be capable of getting past defenders by dribbling and passing, and he will want to score. The hesitant ball-passer will have made way for the self-confident, technically gifted and assertive attacker.

The most important place to make things happen is the opponents' penalty area. This is where matches are decided and it is what happens here that draws the crowds. Every young player should have played attacking soccer in the course of his training, so that he will know what it is. Later, in matches, he must pose a threat when he is in possession of the ball.

Shooting. Pay attention to technique and hitting the ball accurately.

The player in the left-hand goal feeds the balls to the other two players, who shoot as they turn.

1. Shooting

The player in goal feeds the other two, who flick the ball up and shoot as they turn into the other goal.

In modern soccer chances have to be used. As fewer and fewer chances are being created, players must be able to shoot with both feet from any angle and any position in order to score goals. Goals are the name of the game—the reason why fans fill the stands.

What a player does with the chances he gets is decisive. A goal gives a player wings, whereas a missed opportunity can depress the whole team.

Normally speaking, every player ought to be able to shoot well, because scoring goals is the most important thing in the game. In practice, unfortunately, this is not the case: few players can shoot well with both feet and most players need time and space even to shoot with their strong foot.

Shots from the second line are a thing of the past. Professionals, who are able to train all day, are not even capable of a good shot at goal from the second line. This is incomprehensible, because the technique can be learned fairly rapidly merely with two goals and some balls. From this moment on, players must practice shooting every day.

The keepers feed the players, who take the passes and shoot at goal. After each shot, they receive the ball from the other keeper.

The man in goal plays the balls alternately to the right and left side of the man in the middle, who shoots alternately with his right and left foot.

Left: The man in goal plays the ball to the man in the dark shorts; he taps it on to the third player, who shoots. The two in the middle switch roles each time.

The man in goal feeds the other two players, who shoot in turn. The goals can be continually shifted, enabling coaches to vary the type of practice.

1. Shooting

Above: The player behind the goal throws the balls over it and the other shoots.

Left: The man behind the goal plays the balls to the man next to it, who centers first time, and the third player shoots.

The man in goal feeds the balls sideways and the other two players shoot in turn.

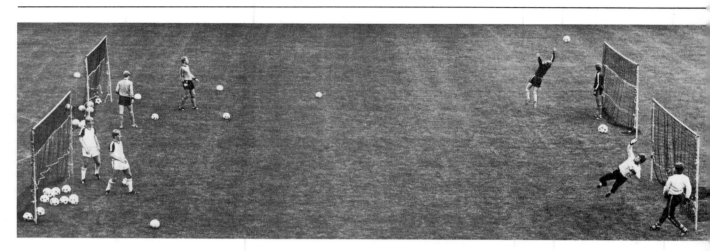

Two players take turns shooting at two keepers, who take turns in goal.

Left: The players behind the goal center and the other two players shoot. Roles are changed when all the balls have been used.

Two players take turns in centering while the other two shoot inside the near post.

1. Shooting

The two players at the sides feed the balls. The three players near the furthest goal shoot in turn.

The players in the goals feed the balls diagonally along the ground or through the air. The other players shoot as they turn.

The players in the side goals feed th balls. The players in the middle shoo on the turn into the center goals.

Left: The players in the side goal feed the balls sideways to the othe players, who shoot from long range

The balls are in the goals in th middle. From there the players do short dribble and shoot.

1. Shooting

The players in the goals with the balls feed them to players running up towards the goal, who shoot, then run behind the goal and then again towards it for their next shot.

The men in the two nearest goals take turns in feeding balls to players coming up, who shoot into the two furthest goals.

The balls are thrown from behind the goals. The four players take turns at heading and constantly change goal.

Heading from a stationary position jumping with both legs.

The keepers throw the balls to the players in a variety of different ways. Three players take turns at heading, moving on to the other group after they have had their turn.

2. Heading

...yers behind the goal throw the ...lls, which two players head, in ...n.

...e players behind the goals throw ... balls diagonally to the other play-..., who head them into the goals.

If the opposing team is playing defensively, the only room left is in the air, which is why heading is becoming increasingly important. More and more goals are the direct or indirect result of duels in the air. English soccer proves that heading duels in the goalmouth are unquestionably spectacular. High balls across the goal are much more exciting to spectators than the endless interpassing that goes on in midfield. Throughout the world huge sums of money are paid for heading specialists, because there are very few players who are good in the air when they are marked by an opponent. These match situations require a realistic form of training, with the players learning to jump with either leg or with both legs together.

Realistic heading training is particularly important for young players because it also develops their jumping power. For this reason the mobile goals shown here are very handy because they can also be used for all sorts of heading games. These goals must be present at all times on any training field in order to allow players to work individually before and after regular sessions.

The keepers throw the balls. The players come in alternately from the right and the left, jumping with their left leg and right leg respectively.

The player at the back lobs the ball over the middle player to the player in the foreground, who heads the ball to the feet of the first player as he runs forward. This player then takes up position at the front.

The player in the foreground lobs the ball for the player at the back, who heads it to the feet of the first player as he runs past the middle player. He then takes up position at the back.

2. Heading

Two players center, the other two head the balls into the goals.

One player (not visible in the photograph) centers and two players go up for the ball, each trying to score. The other two players duel for the next ball.

The players with the balls center them and the other players head them into the goals.

One against one with two neutral players (white shirts). A player who scores retains possession of the ball.

In the foreground, two against two with one neutral player. In the background, three against three, one of the players of the team not in possession acting as goalkeeper.

Four against four with four goals. No handling is allowed and goals can be scored only by heading.

2. Heading

The players in the goals on the left center the balls diagonally. The other players, in twos, compete with each other to head it in.

The men behind the goals throw the balls, which the pairs in the middle try to head in, starting one behind the other and alongside each other.

The keepers throw the balls. Two players take turns in trying to beat the permanent defender in the air, coming in from the right and the left.

The players each get a ball from the keeper (right), beat an opponent and score. They then become defenders and the defenders become the attackers.

Left: The keepers kick the balls over the defenders to the attackers, who make a solo run and score. The keepers at the other end then kick the ball to the defenders, who now become attackers.

Two players in possession beat their opponents and score. The balls are then passed to the defenders, who attack the other goal.

3. Individual play

...vo attackers set out in turns from the ...oal and are opposed by a defender.

...ight: One against one with a neutral ...ssistant to return passes. The player ...ho scores becomes the assistant and ...e assistant becomes the defender.

...he individual moves learned from the ...cond and third phases of the book ...an be used in trying to score. The ...ayer receives a pass with a man ...arking him, and it is then one ...gainst one.

A game's entertainment value for the spectators is determined by *individual* play. Players who are capable of individual initiatives create decisive openings, and when players of this kind cap a solo run with a goal the crowds are really thrilled. In their all-important formative years, young players must become masters of individual play in order to ensure that they do not vanish into the ranks of the nondescript.

There is no more gratifying job for a coach, because there is nothing young players like better than dribbling and scoring. By making one individual play after another, without any conscious effort, players acquire a better grasp of the game and come to realize that individual moves produce more results and more goal opportunities than simply passing the ball to a teammate.

There is no way that players without individual qualities can raise themselves above the rank and file. Outside the penalty area there is ample room for individual play; inside the penalty area fast footwork is essential. As players are being given less and less time and space to shoot and make combinations, the speed with which they act is decisive.

In this section all of the different forms of practice can be used, while the mobile goals can be set up in a variety of arrangements.

Three against three, the object being to score.

Three against three, or four against four, with four goals.

Three against three with three goals, one for one team and two for the other. If there are not enough keepers one member of the team goes in goal.

4. Group games (scrimmages)

The handy thing about goals with straight nets is that two games can be played with three of them.

The players have now mastered all of the techniques needed in this section to create chances and to score. You must have command of all the techniques before playing games with big goals, otherwise they don't have much point. Proof of this is that players are as limited at the end of their careers as they were at the beginning. Though they play year in and year out they cannot develop, because they have not mastered the techniques needed. Once you have command of

Left: Four against four with four goals. There are keepers in two of them. In the other two, goals can only be scored with the head.

Three against three in a demarcated area. A player who crosses the imaginary line shoots as soon as possible.

Three pairs take turns in trying to g
past one another. One pair defenc
the imaginary line. Once this he
been crossed the player must shoot c
quickly as possible. The defende
then receive the ball from the oth
end and become attackers.

Left: Four against four with fon
goals. There are three groups of fou
in total, with the groups taking turn
to provide the keepers.

The same as above, except that now
is three against three with one neutro
player. The winner is the team the
scores the most goals in succession.

4. Group games (scrimmages)

Three groups of three, one group resting while the other two play against each other. The scoring team retains possession.

the techniques and have shot at goal from every angle and position, you can give free play to your creativity in a game.

In every type of game, players must use all of the techniques they have learned and the amount of opposition must gradually be increased. Games with several goals are a particularly good way for players to exercise their powers. If a player in possession persists in playing unimaginatively, the ball is forfeited to the opposing team, because colorless soccer is now definitely taboo.

Three against three with a neutral assistant on the imaginary line.

Four against four. Goals can be scored either by putting the ball into one of the two nets or by dribbling it over the imaginary line. The scoring team retains possession.

Phase Five
Physical Condition

In the fifth phase extra attention is paid to players' physical condition, but all the techniques which have been learned so far are gone through again. The coach decides the intensity, the number of repetitions, the duration and the rest periods.

Condition training is unrealistic almost everywhere. Were this not so, for years now soccer would have been dominated by the East bloc countries. Running and sprinting in accordance with scientific training programs do not make you a soccer personality, merely a superfit player with a minimum of creative technical ability.

Though a soccer coach should have some basic knowledge of physiology, it certainly isn't necessary for him to know the Latin names of all the muscles. What he does need is a thorough knowledge of realistic exercises for increasing the co-ordination, speed, explosive power and stamina of his players. Far too often one sees players being driven about like a herd by a coach's whistle and performing all sorts of exercises in which there is

no trace of independence or personality.

It is perfectly all right to subject technically gifted players to old-fashioned conditioning once in a while, but it is wrong for technically limited players to waste costly time on such soul-destroying routines. Condition training, like other forms of training, must be match-oriented. It must be such that players improve their technical skills and simultaneously develop an optimal condition for playing a game of soccer.

1. Agility and Flexibility

The literature on training is overflowing with unrealistic forms of exercise to develop a player's agility and flexibility. What one sees in practice, however, is that after ten years of such exercises a player is still angular and uneconomical in his movements, which says all that needs to be said about the practicality of the exercises in question.

Even a trained gymnast would look clumsy practicing the ball techniques, because he does not have the necessary coordination. The only way you can acquire the coordination and suppleness needed is by constant training with the ball.

This will give you optimal flexibility in the ankle and hip joints and it will also develop flexibility of the spine (turning). The only joint for which there is an abundance of exercises in the specialist literature is the shoulder joint, which is an area of lesser importance for soccer players.

2. Basic Stamina

In recent years sportsmen have been working on their basic stamina by running ever longer distances, with the emphasis more on duration than on speed and intensity. In this type of training the pulse rate varies between 130 and 140 beats a minute. Heart volume, respiration and blood flow are developed, and these are the things which largely determine *stamina.*

Heart volume is the amount of blood that the heart pumps through the body per minute. The more blood is pumped through the body per minute, the more oxygen is supplied to the muscles and, hence, the more work they can perform. The body also recovers more rapidly from effort. Distance running is unnecessary, because basic stamina can be improved by practicing the ball techniques. What the coach must do is have the players practice the ball techniques in such a way that the heartbeat fluctuates between 130 and 140 per minute. They will then be improving their technical skills as well as their stamina at the same time.

3. Speed

The only problem area as regards developing a player's physical qualities is sprinting speed. For the most part this is inherited. Even an ideal program of sprint training will not give a slow player the speed of a natural sprinter. In soccer, however, speed does not mean sprint speed alone. The main thing a player needs is the ability to make decisive moves in a game, and this is something that any player who follows this training plan can achieve because it will greatly improve his tactical insight. Slow players, therefore, need not despair. There are masses of fast players who cannot make fast, decisive moves for want of the techniques and tactical skills needed for successful ball possession. A dynamic player is capable, when circumstances allow, of rapidly setting constructive moves in motion. A lot of attention needs to be paid to speed, particularly in youngsters between the ages of thirteen and sixteen. All of the exercises can now be practiced at speed and emphasis can also be put on speed in group games. There is no point in training for speed when you haven't yet recovered from your previous exertions. The various exercises and competitive forms of practice should therefore be carried out with three or four players to ensure that they have adequate rest.

4. Stamina and Speed of Play

All the exercises and competitive forms of practice can be used to raise the pulse rate to 170–180 beats a minute. Duration, intensity, number of repetitions and rest periods can be determined by the coach, who can gradually increase the various components.

The enthusiasm among the players will be so great that, contrary to the situation with the usual condition training without a ball, they will need *restraining* rather than encouraging. It is very important that the coach be alert to the fact that young players in

particular must have sufficient rest between exercises. The rest periods can be used for ball exercises requiring little effort. Coaches with a talent for improvisation can put it to good use here.

Right: The players in possession pass the balls to the players on the other side and sprint after them. They repeat this three times (or more).

Four players move around a square, playing the balls past the cones on the inside and sprinting around them on the outside. All kinds of movements can also be practiced at the cones. The players are replaced two at a time by the two that are resting.

Three players with one ball. The first player sprints a certain number of yards with the ball at his feet, stops it and plays it back. The second player does the same. The third player runs half the distance, returns to where he started from and passes the ball across to the first player, who repeats as before.

164

Agility and flexibility

Left: The players with the balls can either pass them back or leave them at the cones and sprint back to their places. Depending on what the first two have done, the second pair either take the balls to the cones or collect them there.

Two groups of three with two balls. The players with the balls sprint to the other side and pass them back. All sorts of variations are possible later. The players in possession can go through all the movements in the middle.

Three players form a square with an unoccupied corner. The two players in possession take turns in playing the ball diagonally to the unoccupied corner, where it is intercepted by the third player. Using the same setup, the player without a ball goes to get it and plays it to the corner he has just left.

The players in possession carry out whichever movement they wish when they reach the defenders and a double movement halfway between two defenders.

One pair receive balls from the other pair and beat their opponents at speed. Balls are then passed to the defenders from the other side and they become attackers.

Agility and flexibility

Two players pass the balls to the other side and cross over at speed to take the places of the players who have received them. Meanwhile, the latter have passed the balls and cross after them.

Left: The players in the foreground have passed the balls. The players in the background receive them and beat the players in the foreground. They then pass the balls back and repeat.

Three players without a ball form a triangle.The three players in possession beat each of them twice by going around them on the outside. Roles constantly alternate, as does the direction in which the players go around the triangle.

The player in possession beats his opponent or places a through pass for the supporting player. The defender receives the ball from the other side and the man without a ball becomes the supporting player.

Right: The players in possession sprint with the ball to the opponents facing them. When they reach their opponents they shield the ball and sprint back with it. The players constantly switch roles.

Below: Four pairs form a large square. One player from each pair goes to collect the ball belonging to the next pair. He then goes around the square in the opposite direction, executing a movement as he goes past each opponent. When he reaches the place where he collected the ball he leaves it there and sprints back to his own place. The other four members of the pairs then do the same thing, and so forth.

Agility and flexibility

The players in light tops make long one-two combinations, then join the other group. After a certain number of minutes the players change roles and those in dark tops make the same combinations.

Three pairs of players beat the permanent defenders in the middle in turn, either by dribbling or by passing.

The players in possession work back and forth between two players. Again, all sorts of variations are possible. The players constantly switch roles.

The players in dark shorts act alternately as defender and one-touch assistants. The players in white engage in individual play or make one-two combinations. Roles switch.

Left: The players in possession beat their opponents, stop the ball, then take up position as defenders, whereupon the other players become attackers.

The two players in white work in turns. They beat the defender, then come back and either beat him again or make a one-two combination with the other player.

Agility and flexibility

Two players in possession sprint in turns into an open space, encounter a defender and beat him.

Two players take turns in beating a defender at speed. The defender operates on an imaginary line.

Left: The two players in dark shorts must defend the imaginary line. After the attackers have made a given number of attempts to beat them, the roles change.

Jump with one leg, land on the other, hop and jump as explosively as possible with the same leg.

The same exercise, but now jump as far sideways as possible.

Jump as explosively as possible with one leg, land on the other, bend the knee and again jump as high as possible using one leg. A variant is to perform the jump as a hop by landing on the jumping leg.

Agility and flexibility

In a zigzag pattern, a cross jump followed by a hop with one leg and then with the other.

Jump as far as possible sideways, bend the knees, then jump with the other leg.

In a zigzag pattern, a short run-up followed by a jump, setting off from each leg alternately, and a heading action.

The soccer world has little experience with power training because, like the various kinds of condition training, it was adapted from other sports. Coaches who argue that power training is not necessary because many top players have never had any forget that these players have natural power. There are other players, however, who could reach the top if they developed explosive power. Preseason power training sessions using modern equipment can do no harm, and it is also very useful to have one session a week during the season. With this training plan power is developed through the innumerable exercises in which explosive action is called for.

Jumping exercises that make use of your own body weight also can be used. If a player makes twenty jumps, setting off ten times from his right leg and ten times from his left, this means that each leg has pushed the weight of his body into the air ten times. The increase in thrust in the two legs will become apparent fairly quickly and this will also improve the player's speed.

Up to the age of twelve the players already jump enough in practicing heading technique. Between the ages of thirteen and sixteen their explosive power and athletic ability can gradually be increased by means of special jumping exercises.

Phase Six
Defensive Qualities

The increase in defensive tactics and the development of players' defensive qualities are disturbing, and the more so because the development of attacking qualities in the players has not kept pace. You can read all about defensive concepts in the specialist literature, but nowhere, unfortunately, can you read how to learn attacking techniques. That is why this training plan is concerned almost entirely with attack. Naturally, attention is also paid to defensive qualities.

for the ball. A technically gifted player has so much control over his body that he is a more effective defender.

The advantage of this training plan is that players who have attacking qualities will want to demonstrate them during a game. A technically strong team wants to hold the opponents in their own half while taking measures to defend against counterattacks. For a technically gifted team this is the best defense. When possession is lost, these players immediately cover. Personalities detest running after an opponent. Permanent man-to-man marking is just as unrealistic as permanent zonal marking. If the defenders also have individual qualities that enable them to beat an opponent, except in the case of the strikers, man-to-man marking will play an increasingly smaller role. Once you have mastered all the attacking techniques, the group games provide all the opportunity you need to master

Defense has played a substantial part in all the competitive forms of practice and group games in the previous phases. You have already learned how to use your body correctly to shield the ball from an opponent when you receive a pass and come away with the ball and in all the exercises and games you have had to defend in a correct manner. The players who survive on the strength of work rate and mentality are constantly engaged in a fight

zonal marking and the organization of a defense.

Sliding tackles

The sliding tackle is the only defensive technique we shall deal with, because if it is carried out with technical perfection the danger of injury is nil for both the defender and the attacker. If you pin your opponents down in their own half, it is

Sliding tackles

Sliding tackle with the outside of the foot, with and without an opponent. The other leg is to the side of the body.

reassuring to have mastered the sliding tackle, because this enables you to play in a line that is flat across the field ready for the offside trap.

There are six ways of carrying out a sliding tackle. The agility and suppleness acquired in the previous phases can be put to good use here. In practicing sliding tackles it is advisable to wear "sliding trousers" made of soft canvas to avoid sliding burns. Though attacking play is what really draws the crowds, a perfectly ex-

Sliding tackle with the sole, with and without an opponent. The other leg is under the body.

..iding tackle with the inside of the ..ot, with and without an opponent, ..e ankle on the ground. The other leg .. to the side of the body.

ecuted sliding tackle will do soccer no harm, because it is part of the many-sidedness of the game.

..ght: "Sliding trousers" of soft can-..s prevent burns.

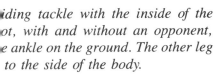

Sliding tackle. Trap the ball with t.
inside of the foot, but not sideways

Sliding tackles

Sliding tackle, with and without opponent. Trap the ball with the inside of the foot trapped. The other leg is bent under the body.

Sliding tackle, with and without opponent. Kick the ball away. The other leg is bent under the body.

Two pairs. The two players perform sliding tackles in which they kick the balls out of the demarcated area. A number of variants are possible. The other two players can play the balls back into the demarcated area or act as opponents.

Phase Seven
Moving With and Without the Ball

The fashionable term "collective play" has scarcely been used so far. Nonetheless, you have been working towards collective play from the very first training session, because without the techniques a player is powerless and for such players to play well collectively is impossible. You must be strong individually to play collectively. For years now the two have been placed in the reverse order, with predictable results.

If you learn all the techniques in youth you will have every opportunity of developing into a soccer personality. In the games with larger groups (5 against 5, 7 against 7, attackers against defenders) the player must have a wide view of what is happening on the field. Moving without the ball becomes important, because everyone knows that the ball determines the tempo. In practice, however, one-touch play is often impossible, particularly in and around the penalty area. Usually you have to get past an opponent in order to create a scoring opportunity. Now that you have mas-

Three against three with two neutral one-touch assistants.

Three against three with three neutral assistants between the cones. Players can score by dribbling the ball over the imaginary line.

tered the techniques for doing this you must make use of them. In addition, you must learn how and when to position yourself in such a way that the man with the ball has opportunities for passing. The coaches will now have enough players capable of putting their ideas into practice, because all the players who have followed this training plan have command of attacking techniques. The positions for which the players are best suited will have become apparent in the course of their training. They must now receive specialized training for those positions. Despite the fact that they are primarily responsible for the team as a whole, the coaches, too, must continue to work on the individual development of the players.

Four against four with two neutral assistants.

Four against four with one neutral player. Players can score by dribbling the ball over the three imaginary lines. When a team has scored it retains possession and players try to score against the other two goals.

Three against three with three neutral assistants.

Moving with and without the ball

Three against three with four neutral assistants.

Three against three with one neutral player.

Four against four with four assistants (the keepers).

A New Generation of Players

I hope we agree by now that youngsters need a coach who can teach them the techniques of the top players. He must also give them the chance to use those techniques in order for them to develop into good players and rise above the ranks of the nondescript.

No training plan can ever be complete. If a trainer, or player, works intensively on the techniques and exercises given here, he will constantly discover or invent new ones and add greater variety to his game.

Through club sessions and homework, after a while the players will begin to taste success. Once they do so, no further encouragement will be needed from the coach, because success acts like a stimulant on a player. The result will be a new generation of players, who no longer wait for the coaches' whistle but practice of their own accord with the ball, think and talk about their development an work on it themselves. In this wa they will acquire the individual, technically creative qualities which a indispensable attributes of an ou standing player.